Unity and Truth

An Ecclesiological Approach to the Church of England's Debate about Human Sexuality

by Martin Davie

The Latimer Trust

The Latimer Trust (formerly Latimer House, Oxford) is a conservative evangelical research organisation within the Church of England, whose main aim is to promote the history and theology of Anglicanism as understood by those in the Reformed tradition. Interested readers are welcome to consult its website for further details of its many activities.

The Latimer Trust
London N14 4PS UK
Registered Charity: 1084337
Company Number: 4104465
www.latimertrust.org
administrator@latimertrust.org

Contents Page

Introduction

The paper on the LLF process from the House of Bishops for the July 2024 meeting of the General Synod has been published under the title *LLF: Moving Forward as One Church* (GS 2358).[1]

In the four chapters that follow I shall not undertake a detailed analysis of the contents of the House of Bishop's document. This task has already been undertaken by Andrew Goddard in his excellent paper 'What is now being proposed for Living in Love and Faith?' which is available on the Psephizo website.[2]

What I shall do instead is review what is being proposed by the House of Bishops as the way forward for the Church of England in the light of what is said by Bishop Martyn Snow in the Preface to the bishops' document, namely, 'Unity matters – it really matters.'[3]

That the bishops as a whole agree with him is shown by the fact that these words are included in the Preface and by the fact that the title of the whole paper is *LFF: Moving Forward as One Church*. The word 'one' indicates that the bishops desire the Church of England to remain united as one church

---

1   The House of Bishops, GS 2358, *LLF: Moving Forward as one Church*, https://www.churchofengland.org/sites/default/files/2024-06/gs-2358-living-in-love-and-faith.pdf.
2   Andrew Goddard, 'What is now being proposed for Living in Love and Faith?', https://www.psephizo.com/sexuality-2/what-is-now-being-proposed-for-living-in-love-and-faith.
3   *LLF: Moving Forward as one Church*, 2.

and are presenting their new proposals as a way to achieve this.

I shall argue two things in my review.

Firstly, what the bishops are proposing as the way forward for the Church of England on the issue of human sexuality is not compatible with a proper theological understanding of what the unity of the Church requires.

Secondly, because this is the case, should the Church of England continue to move in the direction that the bishops are proposing, conservative Christians in the Church of England will have no alternative, but to seek to establish an orthodox third province within the Church of England, precisely as a way to preserve as much unity as possible.

I. What do we mean by the Church?

The various meanings of the word 'church'

In order to understand what sort of unity the Church requires it is first of all necessary to be clear what the term 'church' means.

Writing in the mid-nineteenth century, the evangelical Anglican writer J C Ryle noted that the term 'Church' is one that:

> ... different people use ... in different senses. The English politician in our days talks of 'The Church.' What does he mean? You will generally find he means the Episcopal Church established in his own country. – The Roman Catholic talks of 'the Church.' What does he mean? He means the Church of Rome and tells you that there is no other Church in the world except his own. – The Dissenter talks of 'the Church.' What does he mean? He means the communicants of that chapel of which he is a member. – The members of the Church of England talk of 'the Church.' What do they mean? One means the building in which he worships on a Sunday. Another means the clergy, – and when anyone is ordained, tells you that he has gone into the Church! A third has some vague notions about what he is pleased to call apostolical succession and hints mysteriously that the Church is

made-up of Christians who are governed
by Bishops, and of none beside.[1]

The kind of linguistic confusion to which Ryle refers in this quotation persists to this day. However, it can begin to be alleviated if we are clear that although the word church is used today to refer to a building used for Christian worship and for the various Christian denominations that have emerged over the centuries since the day of Pentecost, neither of these senses is found in the New Testament. Rather, in the New Testament the term church refers to three overlapping sets of people, the Christians who meet together for worship (as in the church meeting in the house of Priscilla and Aquila, Romans 16:5), the Christians in a particular geographical location (as in the 'church in Jerusalem,' Acts 8:1), and the whole body of Christians throughout the world (as in 1 Corinthians 12:28) which is the Church properly so called (what Christian linguistic convention has referred to as the Church with a capital C).

Put into Church of England terms this New Testament usage means that the term 'church' covers the various local Church of England congregations, the forty-two dioceses of the Church of England, the two Church of England provinces of Canterbury and York, and the Church of England as the single, federated, national body made up of these two provinces. All of these are different manifestations of the 'one Catholic and Apostolic Church' referred to in the Nicene Creed. Just as two slices of cheese cut from the same piece of Wensleydale are both pieces of cheese despite the

1   John Ryle, *Knots Untied* (London: Chas. J. Thynne & Jarvis, 1927), 175–176.

difference in size between them, so likewise all these different manifestations of the Church of England are all equally parts of the Church.

The mixed nature of the Church

A further point that is also important to note is that the witness of the New Testament in passages such as Matthew 13:24–30 and 36–43, Matthew 25:14–30 and Revelation 2:18–3:6 further tells us that whether we are talking about a particular worshipping community, or a group of Christians in a particular geographical area, or the Church throughout the world, we need to be aware that the group of people concerned will contain both those who are genuine Christian believers and those who are not.

The distinction between these two different sets of people within the Church is not one that is generally talked about today. However, it is a very important distinction if we are to think rightly about the nature of the Church, because it forces us to think carefully about what the word 'Church' actually means.

The truth that the Church has these two types of people within it was emphasised by Augustine in the fifth century in his book the *City of God*. In this book Augustine uses the term 'City of God' to refer to the body of true Christian believers, and he explains that among her current enemies are those who will in due course become her citizens and, conversely, that there are those who currently appear to be her members who will not be part of God's people in the world to come because in reality they do not belong to the City of God, but to what Augustine elsewhere calls the 'earthly city.'

Augustine writes as follows:

> She [the City of God] must bear in mind that among these very enemies are hidden her future citizens; and when confronted with them she must not think it a fruitless task to bear with their hostility until she finds them confessing the faith. In the same way, while the City of God is on pilgrimage in this world, she has in her midst some who are united with her in participation in the sacraments, but who will not join with her in the eternal destiny of the saints. Some of these are hidden; some are well known, for they do not hesitate to murmur against God, whose sacramental sign they bear, even in the company of his acknowledged enemies. At one time they join his enemies in filling the theatres,[2] at another time they join with us in filling the churches.
>
> But such as they are, we have less right to despair of the reformation of some of them, when some predestined friends, as yet unknown even to themselves, are concealed among our most open enemies. In truth, those two cities are interwoven and intermixed in

---

2   Augustine here assumes that no true Christian would attend a Roman theatre.

this era, and await separation at the last judgement.[3]

What Augustine teaches us here is that the distinction between those who belong to God and will share life with him in eternity and those who do not cuts across the distinction between the Christian Church as an observable religious community and the wider world. There are those in the Church who belong to God's people, those in the Church who do not belong to God's people, and those in the world who do not currently belong to God's people, but who one day will.

The Church visible and invisible

In the sixteenth and seventeenth centuries, Protestant theologians used the terms the 'visible church' and the 'invisible church' to make Augustine's distinction between the mixed religious community consisting of both genuine and merely nominal Christians, and the community, whose precise membership cannot be perceived by us, which consists of those who currently belong to God's people,[4] or who will do so in the future.

Three examples will illustrate this point.

---

3   Augustine, *City of God*, Bk 1:35, trans. Henry Bettenson, ed. David Knowles (Harmondsworth: Penguin, 1981), 45–46.
4   Those who currently belong to God's people include those who have died and who now stand before the throne of God in heaven (see Revelation 7:9–17).

The first is what is said by Thomas Cranmer in his *Thirteen Articles* of 1538.

The Thirteen Articles were a set of doctrinal articles drawn up by Archbishop Thomas Cranmer in connection with discussions that took place between representatives of the German Lutheran Princes and representatives of the Church of England to see if it would be possible to achieve doctrinal agreement between the Lutherans of the Augsburg Confession and the Church of England.

Article 5 of these articles is on 'The Church.' In this article Cranmer writes:

> In the Scriptures the word 'Church' has two main meanings apart from others; one of which means the congregation of all the saints and true believers, who really believe in Christ the Head and are sanctified by his Spirit. This is the living and truly holy mystical body of Christ, but known only to God, who alone knows the hearts of men. The second meaning is that of the congregation of all who are baptized in Christ, who have not openly denied him or been justly and by his word excommunicated. This meaning of 'Church' fits its position in this life in that in it the good are mixed with evil. It must be recognized in order to be heard, as it is written 'Whoever does not listen to the Church', etc. it is discerned by the preaching of the Gospel and the fellowship of the sacraments. This is the

Catholic and Apostolic Church which is not limited to the see of Rome or of any other church, but includes all the churches of Christendom, which together make up the one Catholic (Church).[5]

Cranmer does not use the term 'visible' and 'invisible church' here,[6] but the distinction that he makes in this quotation is nevertheless between these two forms of the Church.

The second is the words of Alexander Nowell in his *Larger Catechism* of 1571, a work which was authorised for educational use by the Church of England.

Nowell distinguishes between the invisible and visible Church as follows. The invisible church, which is the Church principally referred to in the Creed, is:

> ... the congregation of those whom God by his secret election hath adopted to himself through Christ: which church can neither be seen with eyes, nor can continually be known by signs.[7]

---

5   Thomas Cranmer, *The Thirteen Articles*, Article 5 in *Documents of the English Reformation*, ed. Gerald Bray (Cambridge: James Clarke, 1994), 189.
6   This is possibly because Lutherans tended not to use this language.
7   Alexander Nowell, *Nowell's Catechism* (Cambridge: CUP/Parker Society, 1853), 174.

By contrast, the visible church:

> ... is nothing else but a certain multitude of men, which in what place soever they be, do profess the doctrine of Christ, pure and sincere, even the same which the evangelists and apostles have, in the everlasting monuments of holy scriptures, faithfully disclosed to memory, and which do truly call upon God the Father in the name of Christ, and more-over do use his mysteries, commonly called sacraments, with the same pureness and simplicity which the apostles of Christ used and have put in writing.[8]

The third is Richard Hooker's statements about the invisible and visible Church in *The Laws of Ecclesiastical Polity*. Hooker begins Book III of *The Laws of Ecclesiastical Polity*, which was published in 1594, by considering the nature of the Church, and he starts by describing the invisible Church, which he describes as the Church 'mystical':

> That Church of Christ, which we properly term his body mystical can be but one; neither can that one be sensibly discerned by any man, inasmuch as the parts thereof are some in heaven already with Christ, and the rest that are on earth (albeit their natural persons be visible) we do not discern under this property, whereby they are truly and infallibly of that body. Only our minds by intellectual conceit

---

8   Nowell, *Nowell's Catechism*, 174–175.

10

are able to apprehend, that such a real body there is, a body collective, because it containeth a huge multitude; a body mystical, because the mystery of their conjunction is removed altogether from sense. Whatsoever we read in Scripture concerning the endless love and the saving mercy which God sheweth toward his Church, the only proper subject thereof is this Church. Concerning this flock it is that our Lord and Saviour hath promised, 'I give then eternal life, and they shall never perish, neither shall any pluck them out of my hands' [John 10:28]. They who are of this society have such marks and notes of distinction from all others, as are not object unto our sense; only unto God, who seeth their hearts and understandeth all their secret cogitations, unto him they are clear and manifest. All men knew Nathanael to be an Israelite. But our Saviour piercing deeper giveth further testimony than men could have done with such certainty as he did: 'Behold indeed an Israelite in whom is no guile' [John 1:47]. If we profess as Peter did [John 21:15], that we love the Lord, and profess it in the hearing of men, charity is prone to believe all things, and therefore charitable men are likely to think we do so, as long as they see no proof to the contrary. But that our love is sound and sincere, that it cometh from 'a pure heart and a good conscience and love unfeigned' [1 Timothy 1:5], who can pronounce, saving only the Searcher of all men's hearts, who alone intuitively know who in this kind are his?[9]

Hooker then moves on to describe the visible Church, concerning which he writes:

And as those everlasting promises of love, mercy, and blessedness belong to the mystical Church; even so on the other side when we read of any duty which the Church of God is bound unto, the Church whom this doth concern is a sensibly known company. And this visible Church in like sort is but one, continued from the first beginning of the world to the last end. Which company being divided into two moieties, the one before, the other since the coming of Christ; that part, which since the coming of Christ partly hath embraced and partly shall hereafter embrace the Christian Religion, we term as by a more proper name the Church of Christ. And therefore the Apostle affirmeth plainly of all men Christian that be they Jews or Gentiles, bond or free, they are all incorporated into one company, they all make but one body [Ephesians 2:16, 3:6]. The unity of which visible body and Church of Christ consisteth in that uniformity which all several persons thereunto belonging

---

9   Richard Hooker, *Of the Laws of Ecclesiastical Polity*, Bk.III.1.2 in *The Works of Richard Hooker*, Vol.1 (Oxford: OUP, 1841), 276–277.

have, by reason of that one Lord whose servants they all profess themselves, that one Faith which they all acknowledge, that one Baptism wherewith they are all initiated [Ephesians 4:5].[10]

The presence of the visible and invisible Church in the Thirty-Nine Articles and the *Book of Common Prayer*

It is sometimes suggested that the distinction between the visible and invisible Church is not one that is found in the Thirty-Nine Articles or the *Book of Common Prayer*. However, this suggestion is mistaken.

In his book *On the Thirty Nine Articles* Oliver O'Donovan laments what he describes as: 'The disappearance of the invisible church' from the Church of England's Thirty-Nine Articles.[11] He notes that Article XIX of the Articles: 'begins, 'the visible church of Christ...' but never goes on to say anything about the invisible church,'[12] and he contrasts this lacuna in the Articles

> ...with the Westminster Confession, representing the Augustinian mainstream of Protestant thought. Chapter 25 of the Confession begins with a statement about 'the catholic or universal Church, which is invisible,' and then continues in §2 with a further statement about 'the

10   Hooker, *Laws*, Bk III.1.3, 277.
11   Oliver O'Donovan, *On the Thirty Nine Articles* (Exeter: Paternoster Press, 1986), 91.
12   O'Donovan, *Thirty Nine Articles*, 88.

visible Church, which is also catholic or universal under the Gospel.[13]

At first glance, the contrast which O'Donovan draws between the presence of the invisible church in the Westminster confession and its absence in the Thirty-Nine Articles seems convincing. However, the issue is not as simple as he suggests.

Firstly, the very fact that Article XIX refers to 'the *visible* church of Christ' rather than simply to 'the church of Christ' implies the existence of an invisible church of Christ. Otherwise, why add the qualifying adjective?

Secondly, O'Donovan fails to note the significance of what is said in Article XVII of the Thirty-Nine Articles. This article begins with the words:

> Predestination to Life is the everlasting purpose of God, whereby (before the foundations of the world were laid) he hath constantly decreed by his counsel secret to us, to deliver from curse and damnation those whom he hath chosen in Christ out of mankind, and to bring them by Christ to everlasting salvation, as vessels made to honour. Wherefore, they which be endued with so excellent a benefit of God be called according to God's purpose by his Spirit working in due season: they through Grace obey the calling: they be justified freely: they be made sons of God by adoption: they be

---

13   O'Donovan, *Thirty Nine Articles*, 88.

made like the image of his only-begotten Son Jesus Christ: they walk religiously in good works, and at length, by God's mercy, they attain to everlasting felicity.

The existence of the group of people described in these words, the elect 'chosen in Christ out of mankind,' is exactly what the Westminster Confession is talking about when it refers to the invisible church. We know this because as we have seen, chapter XXV of the Confession declares that the invisible church 'consists of the whole number of the elect, that have been, or shall be gathered into one, under Christ the head thereof.' What this means is that, just like the Confession, the Thirty-Nine Articles *do* describe the invisible church, but they do so in a separate Article from that referring to the visible church, and they describe it without using the actual term 'invisible church.'

In similar fashion, the *Book of Common Prayer* describes the invisible church without using the term.

It does this in the collect for All Saints' Day which refers to the fact that God 'hast knit together thine elect in one communion and fellowship, the mystical body of thy Son Christ our Lord.'

It likewise does this in the Communion Service in which the third prayer following the reception of communion begins with the words:

> Almighty and ever-living God, we most heartily thank thee, for that thou dost vouchsafe to feed us, who have duly

received these holy mysteries, with the spiritual food of the most precious Body and Blood of thy Son our Saviour Jesus Christ; and dost assure us thereby of thy favour and goodness towards us; and that we are very members incorporate in the mystical body of thy Son, which is the blessed company of all faithful people; and are also heirs through hope of thy everlasting kingdom, by the merits of the most precious death and passion of thy dear Son.

The need to take both forms of the Church seriously

When thinking about the Church we need to take both forms of the Church equally seriously.

We need to understand that merely belonging to the visible Church is no guarantee that we are rightly related to God and therefore belong to the Church invisible. This is only the case if we truly believe in Christ and take seriously both the grace given to us at our baptism and the promises made at our baptism, thanking God for adopting us as his children in Christ, acknowledging and repenting of our sins, and seeking God's help to live more fully in obedience to him in the future in the power given to us by the Holy Spirit and received sacramentally at Holy Communion.

However, we also need to understand the importance of the visible Church in enabling both ourselves and others to become and remain members of the Church invisible. The reason for its importance is explained by

Chapter XXV of the Westminster Confession when it declares that:

> Unto this Catholic visible Church Christ hath given the ministry, oracles and ordinances of God, for the gathering and perfecting of the saints, in this life, to the end of the world; and doth by his own presence and Spirit, according to his promise, make them effectual thereunto.[14]

The point being made in this quotation is that the means by which people are gathered into, and perfected as members of, the invisible Church during their life on earth, is through the 'oracles and ordinances of God,' what Article XIX of the Thirty-Nine Articles calls the 'pure Word of God' being preached and the 'Sacraments' being 'duly ministered.' It is as the pure Word of God in the Scriptures is preached and the Sacraments of Baptism and Holy Communion are duly ministered, that we learn who God is, what he has done for us, and how should live in return, and receive the spiritual strength we need to live in this way. Furthermore, for the Word to be preached and the Sacraments administered there need to be ministers raised up by God to do both. The visible Church matters because it's where all these things happen. It is the community by means of which the saving work of God in Christ becomes effective in this world.

---

14   *Westminster Confession*, Chapter XXV, in *Creeds of the Churches*, ed. J H Leith, rev. ed (Oxford: Basil Blackwell, 1973), 222.

II. The unity of the Church

In chapter I we noted that there are two forms of the Church. There is the Church invisible consisting of all who are, or who will be, the people who belong to God. There is also the Church visible which is the community that exists in this world and is made up of all those who profess the Christian faith, whether their profession is merely nominal, or reflects a saving relationship with God in Christ and hence membership of the Church invisible. In the words of the *Westminster Confession*, in spite of its mixed nature, the Church visible is 'the house and family of God, out of which there is no ordinary possibility of salvation.'[1] This is because it is the community in which God's word is preached and the sacraments are administered and in which, as a result, sinners are able to enter into, and be sustained in, a saving relationship with God in Christ.[2]

The unity of the invisible and visible Church

In his book *Taking God Seriously* J I Packer writes:

> Christian unity is something distinct from both church union and Christian

---

1   *Westminster Confession*, 222.
2   As the words 'no normal possibility of salvation' in the Westminster Confession suggest we cannot exclude the possibility that God will save in eternity those who do not belong to the visible Church in this life. However, it remains the case that according to the New Testament the only certain means of salvation is through the proclamation of the word and the celebration of the sacraments in the visible Church and the relationship with Jesus Christ that flows from this.

fellowship. Simply and basically, it is the stage of being united to, alive in, and governed by, Jesus Christ our living Lord, in company with all other Christians, past and present, those now with Christ in the heavenly Jerusalem of Hebrews 12:22 and those on earth with us today. As each Christian is in Christ and is one with him, so all Christians are one with each other in and through him. 'Christian' here means, quite specifically, a believer who is born again, knows Christ, is indwelt by the spirit, and seeks to live in love to the glory of the triune God. Christian unity is the active, acknowledged togetherness of all Christian people, who share their supernatural life in their Savior's love and who love each other across all boundaries of race, colour, social standing, and denominational church identity. From this standpoint Christianity is a divine gift and foretaste of heaven and is entirely the fruit of God's grace.[3]

What Packer is describing in this quotation is the unity of the invisible Church. This is a perfect unity between true believers in Christ, which is supernaturally created and sustained by God, that can be neither increased nor diminished, even though it can be experienced subjectively to greater or lesser extent. This is the unity for which Jesus prays in John 17:1–26.

---

3   J I Packer, *Taking God Seriously* (Wheaton: Crossway, 2013), Kindle edition, 57.

The unity of the visible Church, by contrast, is a form of unity which is a work in progress, which can be increased or diminished and which, although it has its roots in the action of God, is also something which has to be produced by the action of human beings.

We can see this point illustrated in Paul's words to the Church in Philippi in Philippians 2:1–2: 'So if there is any encouragement in Christ, any incentive of love, any participation in the Spirit, any affection and sympathy, complete my joy by being of the same mind, having the same love, being in full accord and of one mind.'

In these words, Paul is addressing a visible church, and he is urging the members of that church to take action to create a greater degree of unity between them in the face of the divisions which they are currently exhibiting.

What do we mean by the unity of the visible Church?

In the remainder of this study, I shall be concentrating on the issue of the unity of the visible Church and when thinking about this issue the first thing that needs to be noted is that unity itself is neither good nor bad. Whether unity is a good thing, or a bad thing, depends what sort of unity we are discussing. Two examples will illustrate this point.

The first example is the unity exhibited by a cohesive surgical team consisting of surgeons, anaesthetists, nurses, radiographers and specialist technicians working together to save the life of a critically ill patient. This is a good unity because the end for which they are jointly working, saving the life of the patient, is a morally good one.

The second example is the unity exhibited by a criminal gang working together to raid a jewellers' shop, escape afterwards and fence the stolen jewels. As in the case of the surgical team there is a unity of operation, but this unity is a bad unity because the aim of the activity, stealing and then selling the jewels, is a morally bad one.

This basic point, that there can be both good and bad forms of unity, is something that was stressed by Church of England theologians at the time of the Reformation in the context of their discussion of the unity of the visible Church.

This point is made, for example, by Edwyn Sandys, Archbishop of York, in a sermon which he preached before Queen Elizabeth I on Paul's words in Philippians 2:2–5, his version of which reads as follows:

> Be like minded, having the same love, being of one accord and of one judgment. That nothing be done through contention or vain glory, but that in meekness of mind every man esteem other better than himself. Look not every man on his own things, but every man also on the things of other men. Let the same mind be in you, that was in Christ Jesus.[4]

4   Edwyn Sandys, *Works* (Cambridge: CUP/Parker Society, 1842), 93.

Commenting on what Paul says in these verses, Sandys first stresses the importance of unity between Christians:

> The apostle requireth of us a double unity, in 'religion' and in 'brotherly concord.' Both are so necessary, that the one cannot stand long, if the other fall. Unity in religion is a thing most to be desired. 'What is the worst thing of all others? Dissention. What the best? Unity, peace, and agreement.' Thus thought Gregory. And we read that the gospel had his beginning in unity: 'The multitude of them which believed had one heart and one soul' [Acts 4:32]. Schism had his beginning of dissention: 'I am of Paul, I of Apollos, I of Cephas:' [1 Corinthians 1:12] this was that which rent the church of God in pieces. The church is called the 'kingdom of God;' the 'ark of Noah;' the 'body of Christ;' to teach us that it should be at unity in itself. For a house, a ship, a body divided cannot continue: by themselves they are brought to ruin. Wherefore, together with the blessed apostle, 'I beseech you, brethren, by the name of our Lord Jesus Christ, that ye all speak one thing, and that there be no dissentions among you: but be ye knit together in one mind and in one judgment [1 Corinthians 1:10].[5]

---

5 Sandys, *Works*, 93–94.

He then goes on to contrast true and false unity:

> But we must consider which is true unity. For every agreement is not that concord whereunto we are in this place exhorted. Lucifer with other angels consented together; Eve and Adam and the serpent were all of one mind [Genesis 3:1–6]; so were the builders of the tower of Babel [Genesis 11:1–4]; so [Genesis 19:4] were they of Sodom *a puero usque ad senem*, 'from the child to the man of grey hairs'; so were Dathan and Abiram, with their complices[6] [Numbers 16:1–3]; so were the worshippers of the golden calf [Exodus 32:3–4]; so were the sacrificers in Dan and Bethel; so were Pilate and Herod; so were the Jews that cried with one voice, 'Let him be crucified' and so are they which have joined themselves in holy league with no other intent than those wicked confederates had, of whom the prophet saith, 'They assembled themselves together against the Lord, and against his Christ' [Psalm 2:2]. But it is unity of the Spirit, unity in the truth, unity in Christ and in his gospel, whereunto our apostle here exhorteth us. 'The name of peace is goodly, and the opinion of consent,' saith Hilary, 'is a fair and a beautiful thing': but who doubteth that the linked peace of the church and of the gospel is that peace only which is of Christ, which he spake of to his

6 Accomplices.

apostles after his glorious passion, which he commended at his departure as the pawn[7] of his everlasting commandment. All other peace is no peace indeed. 'Nor is he joined to the church,' saith Cyprian, 'who is severed and sundered from the gospel.' St Paul, moving men to unity in religion, saith, 'This is all one thing;' but he addeth further, 'according to Jesus Christ.' [Romans 15:5] The city whereof the prophet speaketh, which is at unity within itself, must be builded upon the foundation of the apostles and of the prophets. For what a concord is that which is at strife with Christ? Unity must be in verity: 'Thy word is verity' [John 17:17] : in this we must agree. 'Let us not hear: This I say, this thou sayest,' but 'This saith the Lord'. [Augustine]. For unity in religion not grounded upon Christ and his gospel is not concord, but conspiracy.[8]

Sandys makes the same point about true and false unity in a sermon he preached on 2 Corinthians 13:11 in which he says:

One temple was builded for the people of God, one law written by the finger of God, that the church of God might in all things be one. The bond of unity is verity: neither can they be truly one, which are not one in truth. And therefore, although an angel should come from heaven with

---

7   Pledge.
8   Sandys, *Works*, 94–95.

all shew of learning, and all appearance of unspotted and undefiled purity, teaching things contrary to that one truth which you have received, reach him no hand, salute him not in token of consent: unity with him is enmity with God. But if all be builded upon the settled foundation of God's truth, if all be members of one body, servants to one master, soldiers fighting under one banner, children of one and the same father; then is the nature of unity and peace amiable.[9]

The key point made by Sandys in these quotations is that the unity of the visible Church needs to be not just any kind of unity, but a unity based on what he calls 'verity' or 'truth.' By these terms he means the truth that God has revealed to us in Christ and through the Spirit, about who he is, what he has done, and how he calls his human creatures to behave in consequence. What Sandys is saying, and what Christian theology as a whole has traditionally said (as shown by his quotations from Hilary, Cyprian and Augustine), is that the visible Church, and individual churches within it, can only be properly united to the extent to which they accept this truth and order their lives in accordance with it.

The belief that the unity of the visible Church needs to be based on a common understanding and commitment to the truth that God has revealed has continued to be accepted by the Church of England and has been the foundation of its ecumenical policy. This fact is illustrated, for example, by what the

---

9   Sandys, *Works*, 429.

Church of England affirms in the *Reuilly Common Statement* of 1999, a statement agreed by the British and Irish Anglican churches and the French Lutheran and Reformed churches.

In this statement (which was endorsed by General Synod) the Church of England affirms together with its ecumenical partners that:

> ...full visible unity must include:

- A common proclamation and hearing of the gospel, a common confession of the Apostolic faith in word and action. That one faith has to be confessed together, locally and universally, so that God's reconciling purpose is everywhere shown forth. Living this apostolic faith, the Church helps the world attain its proper destiny

- The sharing of one baptism, the celebration of one eucharist and the service of a common ministry (including the exercise of a ministry of oversight *episkope*). This common participation in one baptism, one eucharist and one ministry unites all in each place with all in every place within the whole communion of saints. In every local celebration of the eucharist the Church represents and manifests the community of the universal Church. Through the visible communion the healing and uniting power of the Triune God is made evident amidst the divisions of humankind.

- Bonds of communion which enable the church at every level to guard and interpret the apostolic faith, to take decisions, to teach authoritatively, to share goods and to bear effective witness in the world. The bonds of communion will possess personal, collegial and communal aspects. At every level they are outward and visible signs of the communion between persons who through faith, baptism and eucharist are drawn into the kingdom of the Triune God. This communion must have practical consequences, in particular a common engagement of the churches in service and mission.[10]

In this quotation the unity of the visible Church has sacramental, ministerial and organisational aspects, but these aspects of unity are instrumental rather than foundational. They are ways of safeguarding, proclaiming, and living out the truth of the apostolic faith (the revelation given by Christ to the apostles and through them to all subsequent generations of the Church), a faith which everyone in the visible Church is called to confess together (and therefore must hold in common).

The vision of visible unity held by the Church of England and reflected in the words of the *Reuilly Common Statement* is not an idiosyncratic one. Not only does it reflect the historic position of the Christian Church (as we have seen), but it also reflects the contemporary understanding of visible unity

---

10 *Called to Witness and Service* (London: CHP, 1999), 21–22.

that was developed by the worldwide ecumenical movement during the twentieth century.

The classic expression of this understanding is the New Delhi statement on Christian unity agreed by the World Council of Churches in 1961. The second paragraph of this statement declares:

> We believe that the unity which is both God's will and his gift to his Church is being made visible as all in each place who are baptized into Jesus Christ and confess him as Lord and Saviour are brought by the Holy Spirit into one fully committed fellowship, holding the one apostolic faith, preaching the one Gospel, breaking the one bread, joining in common prayer, and having a corporate life reaching out in witness and service to all and who at the same time are united with the whole Christian fellowship in all places and all ages in such wise that ministry and members are accepted by all, and that all can act and speak together as occasion requires for the tasks to which God calls his people.

As in the Reuilly Statement, the unity described in the New Delhi Statement has various aspects, among which are baptism, a shared celebration of Holy Communion, common prayer, a commonly accepted ministry and a common life of witness and service. However, underlying all these various aspects of unity lies 'holding the apostolic faith.' Everything else follows from this. For New Delhi, the visible unity willed by God is the existence of 'one fully committed fellowship, holding the one apostolic faith and preaching the one Gospel.'[11]

Where can truth be found?

If we accept that the unity of both the visible Church as a whole, and individual churches within it, needs to be based on an acceptance of the truth about who God is, what he has done, and how he calls his human creatures to behave in response, this begs the question 'Where can this truth be found?'

As Canons A5 and C15 make clear, the answer that the Church of England gives to this question is that this truth is to be found in what Christian theology refers to variously as 'the faith,' 'the apostolic faith' (as in the Reuilly and New Delhi statements) and 'the faith of the church,' terms which all refer to the authoritative teaching about Christian belief and behaviour that was first handed down by the apostles (see for example Acts 2:42, Romans 6:17, 2 Thessalonians 2:15, Hebrews 10:23, 1 Peter 1:25 and Jude 3) and that has been taught, believed and confessed by orthodox Christians ever since.

The Church of England further teaches that there are three sources for our knowledge of 'the faith.'

The primary source of our knowledge of the faith is the Scriptures of the Old and New Testament in which

---

11 The World Council of Churches, *New Delhi Statement on Unity*, 1961 at: https://www.oikoumene. org/resources/documents/new-delhi-statement-on-unity#:~:text=We%20believe%20that%20.

the Christian faith is witnessed to in words inspired by God himself (2 Timothy 3:16, 2 Peter 1:21). In the words of the Homily 'A fruitful exhortation to the reading and knowledge of Holy Scripture' in the *First Book of Homilies*:

> ... In holy scripture is fully contained, what we ought to do, and what to eschew, what to believe, what to love, and what to look for at God's hands at length. In these books, we shall find the Father, from whom, the Son by whom, and the Holy Ghost, in whom, all things have their being and conservation; and these three Persons to be but one God, and one substance. In these books, we may learn to know ourselves, how vile and miserable we be; and also to know God, how good he is of himself; and how he communicateth his goodness unto us, and to all creatures. We may learn also in these books, to know God's will and pleasure, as much for this present time is convenient for us to know.[12]

The second source is the orthodox Fathers and Councils of the Patristic Period (which the Church of England has traditionally understood to mean the first five centuries of the Church's existence) and the three Catholic Creeds (the Apostles, the Nicene and the Athanasian) which reflect the teaching produced

---

12   *The First Book of Homilies*, 'A fruitful exhortation to the reading and knowledge of Holy Scripture', in *The Homilies*, ed. Ian Robinson (Bishopstone: Brynmill Press and Preservation Press, 2006), 5.

by the Orthodox Fathers and Councils during this period. The Fathers, the Councils and Creeds have a secondary, derived, authority because their authority is dependent on the fact that they bear a faithful witness to the apostolic faith as this is taught in the Scriptures. They are authoritative precisely because they point us beyond themselves to the witness of Scripture.

The third source is the three 'historic formularies' produced by the Church of England during the sixteen and seventeenth centuries, the Thirty-Nine Articles of 1571 and the 1662 *Book of Common Prayer* and Ordinal. The historic formularies bear a tertiary witness to the apostolic faith in the sense that they witness to the Scriptures as read with in the light of the witness of the Fathers, the Councils and the Creeds. Like the writings of the Patristic period, the formularies have a derived rather than an intrinsic authority, but in their case this authority has a double derivation.[13]

At this point someone might object: 'But what about natural theology and the use of reason?' The answer is that their omission is deliberate, and it is due to the fact that neither natural theology nor reason are sources for our knowledge of the faith in the same way as the Scriptures, the Patristic witness or the historic formularies.

The Church of England has traditionally given an important role to natural theology in its apologetics

13 For more on these three sources of Anglican theology see Martin Davie, *Deep Roots: A Beginner's Guide to the Doctrine of the Church of England* (London: Latimer Trust, 2023).

as a way of showing that the faith is congruent with our general knowledge of the world.[14] However, it has not derived its knowledge of the faith from natural theology because while natural theology can show us may important things such as, for instance, that God exists, that he is the ultimate source of our awareness of good and evil, and that human beings can only find their true fulfilment beyond this world, it cannot tell us those things that are at the heart of the Christian faith, what Richard Hooker calls 'those hidden mysteries that reason could never have been able to find out.'[15] It cannot tell us that the creator God is the God of Abraham, Isaac and Jacob who has fulfilled his promises to Israel by becoming incarnate in Jesus Christ and dying and rising again for our salvation. It cannot tell us that Jesus has ascended to God's right hand, that he has poured out the Holy Spirit on his people and that he will come in glory to judge the living and dead and to fully and finally bring in God's kingdom.

If we ask about the role of reason in relation to our knowledge of the faith, the answer is that it has a twofold role.

Firstly, the term 'reason' can mean our God-given capacity for rational thought and when this is illuminated by the Holy Spirit, it can show us that it is rational to believe that the faith is to be found in the threefold witness of the Bible, the writings of the

---

14   Two classic examples of Church of England natural theology are J. Butler, *The Analogy of Religion* (London: Dent, 1936) and William Temple's two works *Mens Creatrix* and *Christus Veritas* (London: Macmillan, 1949).
15   Richard Hooker, *Laws*, Bk I:15:4.

Patristics and the historic formularies and enable us to understand what this witness means.

Secondly, 'reason' can be used to refer to what the *Virginia Report* calls the 'mind of a particular culture,' with its characteristic ways of seeing things, asking about them and explaining them'.[16] When reason is used in this sense we have to take reason seriously in the sense of taking seriously the apologetic task of showing how the Apostolic faith relates to the beliefs and concerns of a particular culture or sub-culture in order to enable those who belong to that culture to understand the faith more clearly.[17]

However, in neither of these roles does reason act as a source for our knowledge of the faith.

Faith and doctrine

The Greek word *didache* (teaching) used by St. Paul in Romans 6:17 was translated in Latin as *doctrina* and from there into English as 'doctrine.' Thus, the Authorized Version of Romans 6:17 talks about 'that form of doctrine' to which the Romans were committed. This linguistic development meant that the term doctrine came to be used in English to refer to the understanding of the Apostolic faith held (and therefore taught) by the Christian church as a whole, or by particular churches within it.

16 'The Virginia Report' in *The Official Report of the Lambeth Conference 1998* (Harrisburg: Morehouse Publishing, 1999), 244.
17 It was because the Church of England lay theologian C. S. Lewis did this so effectively in *Mere Christianity* and other works that he was and remains such a successful Christian apologist.

It is this meaning of the term doctrine that underlies what is said about 'the doctrine of the Church of England' in Canon A5. This is shorthand for the understanding of Apostolic faith held by the Church of England and means the same as 'the faith' which the Church of England 'professes' in Canon C15.

It is the fact that 'the faith' and 'doctrine' mean the same thing that makes sense of the Church of England's insistence that its liturgy must be in accordance with its doctrine. The Church of England holds that the visible Church cannot lawfully 'ordain anything that is contrary to God's Word written' (i.e Scripture).[18] It also believes that its doctrine is in line with the apostolic faith taught in Scripture. Therefore, the fact that the Church of England cannot rightly authorise any liturgical development that is contrary to Scripture must necessarily mean that it cannot rightly authorise any liturgical development that is contrary to its doctrine.

The development of doctrine

A further objection that might be raised at this point is that I have ignored that fact that doctrine develops. 'Surely' it will be said 'we have to see doctrine as something that is dynamic rather than static and which allows us to say new things today that have not been said in the past?'

This objection is valid in so far as it calls attention to the fact that doctrine develops. However, it is invalid in so far as it involves the idea that the development of doctrine involves saying new things. This is mistaken,

18   Article XX.

because legitimate doctrinal development, because it is dependent upon the truth revealed once for all in Scripture, cannot say anything new. What it can and should do is say the same truth in a new way.

The recognition of this fact is often attributed to the nineteenth-century theologian John Newman in his *Essay on the Development of Doctrine*.[19] However, this point has in fact been recognised as far back as the Patristic period. We can see this if we look at what was said by the fifth-century theologian Vincent of Lerins in his *Commonitorium* or *Reminder* in which he addresses the question of whether there can be doctrinal development in the Church.[20]

At first sight his answer to this question would appear to be 'No.' Thus in what has come to be known as the Vincentian canon, or rule, he declares 'in the Catholic church all care must be taken so we hold that which has been believed everywhere, always, and by everyone.'[21] If taken literally this rule would seem to say that any kind of doctrinal development is impossible and the problem which this raises (and of which Vincent was well aware) was that if this is true it rules out orthodox formulations of faith such

---

19   John Newman, *An Essay on the Development of Doctrine* (London: James Toovey, 1846).

20   The full title of Vincent's work is the *Commonitorium peregrini adverse haereticos* (*Reminder of the Pilgrim against the Heretics*). The excerpts from the *Commonitorium* that follow are taken from Thomas Guarino, *Vincent of Lerins and the Development of Christian Doctrine* (Grand Rapids: Baker Academic, 2013).

21   *Commonitorium*, 2.5 in Guarino, *Vincent of Lerins*, 4.

as the Nicene Creed which have not been believed 'everywhere, always and by everyone.'

However, Vincent himself goes on to tell us that this rule should not be taken literally because in fact there can be legitimate progress in Christian theology that leads people to say things that are perfectly orthodox but which have not been said before. Thus, in chapter 23 of the *Commonitorium* he writes:

> But someone will perhaps say: is there no progress of religion in the Church of Christ? Certainly there is progress, even exceedingly great progress [*plane et maximus*]! For who is so envious of others and so hateful toward God as to try to prohibit it? Yet it must be an advance [*profectus*] in the proper sense of the word and not an alteration [*permutatio*] in faith. For progress means that each thing is enlarged within itself [*res amplificetur*], while alteration implies that one thing is transformed into something else [*aliquid ex alio in aliud*]. It is necessary, therefore, that understanding, knowledge, and wisdom should grow [*crescat*] and advance [*proficiat*] vigorously in individuals as well as in the community, in a single person as well as in the whole church, and this gradually in the course of ages and centuries. But the progress made must be according to its own type, that is, in accord with the same doctrine, the same

meaning, and the same judgement [*eodem sensu eademque sententia*].[22]

The point that Vincent is making in this second quotation is helpfully expounded by Thomas Guarino in his book on Vincent's thought. Guarino writes that for Vincent:

> Christian teaching is alive and dynamic... always growing and developing, although with the growth and change that must be organically and architectonically related to that which preceded it. God continues to work in history guiding the church to a fuller understanding of revealed truth, just as God guides natural human realities. This is the point of instance analogies of a child growing into an adult and the seeds becoming a fully formed plant.[23]

However, in line with his first rule Vincent also insists that Christian teaching must always have the 'same meaning' (*idem sensus*):

> The term is decisive because Vincent insists that over the course of the centuries, Christian doctrine must protect the original meaning found in Scripture and the early councils. A continual danger is that, under the guise of development, the meaning of the church's faith is illegitimately

---

22 *Commonitorium*, 23.1–3, in Guarino, *Vincent of Lerins*, 15.
23 Guarino, *Vincent of Lerins*, 17.

transformed, allowing heterogeneous ideas to be introduced. Precisely this kind of alteration constitutes the pernicious adulterations of religion that Vincent labels a *permutatio fidei*. If the substantial content of Christian faith and doctrine is changed, one engages not in the development of the faith but its corruption. Such alteration is no longer *res amplificetur*, doctrine growing within itself; instead, it is a monstrous deformation of Christian belief.

In its objective sense, then, *idem sensus* (*eodem sensu eademque sententia*) intends the continuity of meaning existing over the course of time. Authentic growth can never bespeak the reversal of a fundamental (conciliar) teaching. One may not 'contravene the landmarks' (Proverbs 22:28) that have been established by the fathers.[24]

What Vincent's comments help us to understand is that the unity in truth that the visible Church must seek to maintain allows for the development of Christian teaching down the centuries. However, what it does not allow for is a change in that teaching which contradicts the revelation that the Church has been given by God. The key biblical text cited by Vincent in this regard is 1 Timothy 6:20 'O Timothy, guard what has been entrusted to you.' Taking this text seriously means that an alteration in the basic content of the Church's teaching has to be regarded

---

24   Guarino, *Vincent of Lerins*, 19.

as a failure to maintain unity in truth. You cannot guard what has been entrusted to you by replacing it with something else.

To quote Vincent one last time: 'The Church's task is to consolidate and strengthen doctrine, to guard what has already been confined and defined.'[25] It is because the Church of England has taken this point on board that it has historically insisted (and officially continues to insist) that its doctrine is in line with the teaching of Scripture, the Patristic period and the historic formularies, and that any development of its teaching must reflect this fact (that is why its ministers have to be willing to declare their loyalty to this 'inheritance of faith' as their 'inspiration and guidance under God in bringing the grace and truth of Christ to this generation').[26]

The issue of diversity

Just as unity in truth does not preclude development in doctrine, so also it does not preclude diversity in practice. The legitimacy of such diversity alongside unity in truth is affirmed in Church of England terms in Article XXXIV of the Thirty-Nine Articles which states:

---

25 *Commonitorium 23:17* in Guarino, *Vincent of Lerins*, 22.
26 Canon C15.1. It is important to note that the whole purpose of the English Reformation was not to innovate but to conserve. What the Anglican reformers were attempting to achieve was to restore the godly teaching and practice of the Scriptures and early church by removing the innovations introduced during the Middle Ages and to protect this teaching and practice against the innovations proposed by radical Protestant groups.

It is not necessary that Traditions and Ceremonies be in all places one, or utterly like; for at all times they have been divers, and may be changed according to the diversity of countries, times, and men's manners, so that nothing be ordained against God's Word.

The key point to grasp here is that the final clause qualifies the rest of the statement. Diversity of practice within the visible Church is legitimate, but diversity of practice that permits things that go against the teaching of Scripture is not.

This same point is reflected in the Reuilly statement. This declares:

Full visible unity should not be confused with uniformity: unity in Christ does not exist in spite of and in opposition to diversity, but is given with and in diversity. Both the unity and diversity of the church are grounded in the Triune God, who is perfect communion in diversity. Diversities which are rooted in the biblical witness, theological traditions, spiritualities, liturgies and expressions of ministry, and in various cultural, ethnic or historical contexts, are integral to the nature of communion. Yet there are limits to diversity. Diversity is illegitimate when, for instance, it makes impossible the common confession of Jesus Christ as God and Saviour the same yesterday, today and forever (Hebrews

13:8). Diversity is illegitimate when it denies salvation through Christ and the final destiny of humanity as proclaimed in Holy Scripture, preached by the apostolic community and celebrated in the liturgy of the church.[27]

Once again diversity is affirmed, but it is limited to what is in accordance with the biblical witness, otherwise it is illegitimate.

Furthermore, because the Church of England holds that the orthodox teaching of the Patristic period and the contents of the historic formularies are in agreement with Scripture, diversity of practice that allows things that go against the teaching they contain is likewise illegitimate. It too is a breach of unity in truth.

---

27   *Called to Witness and Service*, 23.

III. Assessing what the bishops are proposing in GS 2358

Where we have got to so far

Where we have got to in chapters I and II can be summarised by the following bullet points:

- The bishops have insisted that 'Unity matters – it really matters'.

- There are two forms of the Church, the Church invisible and the Church visible.

- In the Church visible there can be true and false forms of unity.

- The true unity which the visible Church is called to exhibit is unity in the truth, and the truth concerned is the truth about who God is, what God has done and how God calls his human creatures to behave in consequence, that God has revealed in Christ and through the Spirit.

- The Church of England holds that we know about this truth ('the faith') primarily through the inspired word of God in the Scriptures and secondly through the teaching of the orthodox Fathers, Creeds and Councils of the Early Church and thirdly through the Church of England's 'historic formularies' (the Thirty-Nine Articles, the *Book of Common Prayer* and the 1662 Ordinal).

- The Church of England grounds its doctrine on these three sources and holds that its doctrine is to be accepted because of its fidelity to the truth taught by them. It is because this is the case that any forms of liturgical practice that are contrary to the Church of England's doctrine are ruled out.

- There can be both theological development and diversity of practice within the visible Church, but such development and diversity is limited by the need to be faithful to inheritance of orthodox faith which has been passed on across the centuries since the time of the apostles.

What all this means is that taking seriously the bishops' declaration that 'unity matters' involves testing what they propose regarding the next steps in the LLF proposal against the criterion of unity in truth that has just been outlined. We shall now go on to consider how what they propose measures up against this criterion.

Does what the bishops are proposing meet the criterion of unity in truth?

When considering what the bishops are proposing, it has to be noted first of all that what the bishops propose has a specific starting point. In the 'Overview of key elements' section at the start of GS 2358 the bishops declare: 'Underpinning the proposal is the recognition that, as Christians, we hold a variety of views on LLF, all of which are held with integrity and all of which deserve respect'.[1]

---

1   *LLF: Moving Forward as one Church*, 5.

There are two points that need to be noted about what the bishops say here.

Firstly, the bishops do not explain (a) what it means to hold views with integrity and (b) how they know that all the different views on LLF held within the Church of England are held with integrity. This is simply rhetoric without content.

Secondly, the bishops also fail to explain why all views held with integrity deserve respect. If we assume that holding views with integrity means something like genuinely believing something to be correct, it is easy to see that there can be many beliefs held with integrity that should not be treated with respect.

For example, someone might in all sincerity hold that the world is flat, and the moon made of blue cheese. We might respect the sincerity of that person's belief, but it would be impossible to accept this belief as worthy of respect as a truthful statement about the nature of the world or the moon.

For a more serious example, there is no doubt that the bishops would not say that because a racist belief in white supremacy was held 'with integrity' it should therefore be treated with respect in the Church of England. They would instead rightly say that it should be rejected by all good Anglicans as incompatible with the Christian belief in the equal value of all human beings in the sight of God.

In similar fashion we cannot simply say without more ado that all beliefs held in the Church of England with regard to marriage and human sexuality deserve respect. We have to test them against the Church of England's sources of doctrine and on that basis decide whether they deserve respect. The bishops are therefore proceeding from a mistaken starting point.

When we go on to look at the specifics of what they propose we find that this is equally problematic. What the bishops are proposing to Synod in GS 2358 are three key things:

- The existing form of prayers of blessing for same-sex couples should continue.

- Standalone services of blessing for same-sex couples should be introduced.

- General Synod should support a timetable for deciding whether those who are in same-sex civil marriages are to be ordained and serve as Church of England ministers.

An examination of these three proposals shows that the view that they represent legitimate developments in the life of the Church of England does not deserve respect. This is because the proposals go against the doctrine of the Church of England and as such are contrary to the maintenance of unity in truth.

The blessing of same-sex couples

In the body of GS 2358 the bishops do not explain why they regard the proposals to allow the blessing of same-sex couples, either in normal Sunday services, or in special stand-alone services, as ones that are consonant with the doctrine of the Church of England.

However, in Annex C they repeat the argument put forward previously in GS 2328 in November 2023:

> The PLF[2] are a type of legitimate pastoral provision whereby the Church recognises the reality of people's lives and seeks to respond in ways that affirms what is good, and pray for growth towards God ...

> We consider that the essential doctrines of the Church of England are safeguarded. The PLF do not seek to simulate marriage or pretend that the Church has made a decision to extend marriage to same-sex couples. But they do discern and affirm what is good and pray for God's presence and blessing over the people within the relationship.

> We have therefore come to the view that, in so far as making the PLF available for couples in an active sexual relationship does involve any departure from doctrine, it nevertheless does not involve a departure from doctrine 'in any essential matter,' and that doing so is compatible with the relevant canonical requirements.[3]

---

2   PLF stands for 'Prayers of Love and Faith,' the prayers for use with same-sex couples produced by the bishops in January 2023. These prayers can be found at: https://www.churchofengland.org/sites/default/files/2023-12/prayers-of-love-and-faith.pdf
3   *LLF: Moving Forward as one Church*, 28, 30.

The bishops' argument has three elements to it:

1. The existing and proposed forms of prayer for same-sex couples are not contrary to the doctrine of the Church of England in that they do not say that same-sex couples are married or that God approves of sexual intimacy outside heterosexual marriage.

2. It would be difficult to say that these forms of service are not indicative of a departure from the Church's previous teaching that prayers should not be offered for same-sex couples whose relationships are, or might be, of a sexual nature.

3. Although the forms of service are a development of Anglican practice, they are not indicative of a departure from the Church's doctrine in any 'essential matter' (something that is legally prohibited in Canons B2.1, B4.2 and B5.3), since all they are doing is recognising the 'goods' or virtues that can be found in same-sex relationships and asking for God's blessing that these goods may increase.

What the bishops are trying to do is to bypass the deep disagreement in the Church of England about same-sex marriage and same-sex sexual activity by suggesting that, even if we disagree about such matters, we can (and should) still recognise the goods that exist in same-sex relationships and pray that these goods may increase.

The first thing to note in response to this argument is that it is not only difficult, but impossible, to argue that what the bishops are proposing is not a departure from the teaching contained in the bishops' statements concerning Civil Partnerships and same-sex marriages in 2005, 2014 and 2019.[4] In these statements the bishops said that public prayers should not be said for same-sex couples. What is now being proposed is that such prayers should be offered. If the bishops' previous teaching constitutes Church of England doctrine, or gives expression to it, then what is proposed is contrary to the doctrine of the Church of England.

What the bishops are arguing is that the departure from previous teaching that they propose is not indicative of a change in any 'essential matter' because they are not proposing any change to the Church's doctrine of marriage, or its doctrine of sexual ethics which says that sexual intercourse should only take place within marriage (meaning a marriage with two people of the opposite sex). These doctrines would remain unchanged.

Where their argument falls is that if the Church of England's doctrines of marriage and sexual ethics are viewed alongside the Church's doctrine concerning the need for repentance and forgiveness for sin, then

---

4   The House of Bishops, 'Civil Partnerships: A pastoral statement from the House of Bishops of the Church of England,' 2005, 'Statement of Pastoral Guidance on Same Sex Marriage,' 2014, and 'Civil Partnerships: for same sex and opposite sex couples. A pastoral statement from the House of Bishops of the Church of England,' 2019.

what they are proposing *is* necessarily a change of doctrine in an 'essential matter.'

To understand why this is the case, the point that has to be grasped is that it is an absolutely essential part of Church of England doctrine (as it has been part of the doctrine of the Church as whole) that in order for people to be rightly related to God in this life and eternally happy with him in the next, they have to acknowledge, repent of, and confess their sins, not only in private but in the context of public worship, so that their sins may be forgiven and no longer constitute a barrier between them and God.

According to the doctrine of the Church of England not only does marriage have to be between two people of the opposite sex, and sex to be confined to marriage thus defined, but actions by human beings that are contrary to these two points are sinful.

We can see this in the case of marriage in the words spoken by the priest to the couple seeking to be married at the beginning of the marriage service in the *Book of Common Prayer*:

> I require and charge you both, as ye will answer at the dreadful day of judgement, when the secrets of all hearts shall be disclosed, that if either of you know any impediment, why ye may not be lawfully joined together in Matrimony, ye do now confess it. For be ye well assured, that so many as are coupled together otherwise than God's Word doth allow are not

joined together by God; neither is their
Matrimony lawful.

What is lawful here is what is lawful according to
God's law made known in God's Word in Scripture,
and what the priest is warning the couple is that if
their relationship is not lawful by this standard then
this is a sin for which they will have to answer to God
'at the dreadful day of judgement.'

In the case of sex outside marriage, the marriage
service also states that the second reason marriage
was ordained was: '... for a remedy against sin, and to
avoid fornication; that such persons as have not the
gift of continency might marry, and keep themselves
undefiled members of Christ's body.' What is made
clear here is that fornication is a sin which spiritually
defiles people.

In similar fashion the Litany in the Prayer Book
includes the prayer, 'From fornication, and all other
deadly sin; and from all the deceits of the world,
the flesh, and the devil, Good Lord, deliver us.' Here
fornication is unequivocally described as a 'deadly
sin,' a form of activity that will lead to spiritual death.
If we ask what fornication means, the answer is
that like the New Testament term *porneia* it means
all forms of sexual activity outside heterosexual
marriage. That this is the case is shown in the Homily
'Against whoredom and uncleanness' in the *First
Book of Homilies* in which adultery, whoredom and
fornication are used synonymously to refer to extra
marital sexual activity:

And that ye may perceive, that fornication and whoredom, are in the sight of God most abominable sins, ye shall call to remembrance, this commandment of God, *Thou shalt not commit adultery* (Exodus 20:14). By the which word adultery, although it be properly understood of the unlawful commixtion (or joining together) of a married man with any woman beside his wife, or of a wife, with any man beside her husband: yet thereby is signified also all unlawful use of those parts which be ordained for generation. And this one commandment forbidding adultery, doth sufficiently paint and set out before our eyes the greatness of this sin of whoredom and manifestly declareth how greatly, it ought to be abhorred of all honest and faithful persons. And, that none of us shall think himself excepted from his commandment, whether we be old or young, married or unmarried, man or woman, hear what God the Father saith by his most excellent Prophet Moses: *There shall be no whore among the daughters of Israel, nor no whoremonger among the sons of Israel* (Deuteronomy 23:17).

Here is whoredom, fornication and all uncleanness, forbidden to all kinds of people all degrees, and all ages without exception.[5]

---

5 *The First Book of Homilies*, 'Against whoredom and uncleanness' in Robinson, *The Homilies*, 88–89.

Seen from this perspective all forms of same-sex sexual activity are forms of fornication because, as Paul makes clear in Romans 1:26–27, they involve 'unlawful use of those parts which be ordained for generation.'

If it is indeed the case, as these Anglican doctrinal sources make clear, that both unlawful forms of marriage and same-sex sexual activity are very serious forms of sin, it follows that according to the Church of England doctrine noted above they have to be met with a call to repentance, which in turn needs to be followed by confession and absolution. This point was properly recognised in the motion passed by General Synod in 1987 (the 'Higton motion') which has never been abolished or superseded, and which remains an authoritative statement of the position of the Church of England. This motion declares that like fornication and adultery, 'homosexual genital acts' are to be met 'with a call to repentance and the exercise of compassion' (the two seen as belonging together).[6]

The Prayers of Love and Faith as set out in GS 2328 (which are the ones the bishops are proposing should be used in Church of England Services) make absolutely no reference to repentance (with the sole exception of the general confession at the start of the proposed service of Holy Communion in Annex D). There is no call to those who are in same-sex marriages or same-sex sexual relationship to repent

---

6   The Higton motion can be found in *General Synod Report of Proceedings*, Vol.18, No.3 (London: CHP, 1987), 995–6.

of these forms of sin, no opportunity for confession of them, and no opportunity for absolution.[7]

The question this raises is whether the bishops believe:

a. That same-sex marriages and same-sex sexual activity are not sinful,

or

b. That they are sinful, but that a call to repentance, confession and absolution are not required.

The absence of any call for repentance, any opportunity for confession, or any opportunity for absolution, point to either (a) or (b) being true and are thus indicative of a departure from the doctrine of the Church of England on essential matters.

The key theological point that the bishops have chosen to ignore is that while those in same-sex marriages and same-sex sexual relationships may indeed exercise virtue in these relationships, they have chosen to exercise virtue in the context of forms of relationship which according to Church of England doctrine (and also the traditional doctrine of the whole of the visible Church and the teaching of Holy Scripture) are not virtuous but sinful and therefore need to be met with a call to repentance, leading to confession and absolution (and subsequently amendment of life).

---

7 These prayers can be found at GS 2328, Annexes B–D at https://www.churchofengland.org/sites/default/files/2023-10/gs-2328-llf-nov-2023.pdf.

This theological point is helpfully made by the Roman Catholic Bishop Athanasius Schneider in an article criticising the recent proposal in the Roman Catholic Church to allow the blessing of same-sex couples:

> By blessing a homosexual couple, a cleric neglects his duty to call homosexuals to repentance, and undermines his duty to call to repentance, with due pastoral love, not only same-sex couples but all those who commit sexual sins, and those who live in a state of sexual sin. 'Blessing' the state of sin reinforces the erroneous moral convictions of sinners, and puts them at ease with their sin, causing them to be less likely to repent. Therefore, those who support such blessings de facto encourage same-sex couples to pursue their sinful lifestyle, for which God will condemn them. Those who authorize the 'blessing' of same-sex couples bear the burden and responsibility for the grave spiritual harm caused to these persons. Therefore, such 'blessings' fit the traditional definition of scandal, for they lead others into sin.[8]

In terms of the argument of Vincent of Lerins looked at earlier, it follows that what the bishops are proposing in GS 2358 is not a legitimate development.

---

8   Bishop Athanasius Schneider, 'The Problem of Blessing Same-Sex Couples,' *Crisis Magazine*, 17 June 2024 at https://crisismagazine.com/opinion/the-problem-of-blessing-same-sex-couples-and-its-consequences-for-the-doctrine-and-life-of-the-catholic-church.

To quote Guarini again, the point that Vincent makes is that 'if the substantial content of Christian faith and doctrine is changed, one engages not in the development of the faith but its corruption. Such alteration is no longer *res amplificetur*, doctrine growing within itself; instead, it is a monstrous deformation of Christian belief.' It is such a monstrous deformation of Christian belief that the bishops have already introduced and are proposing should now be developed further. Such a deformation is incompatible with that unity in truth that proper Christian unity requires and therefore shows that they failed to take seriously their professed belief that unity really matters.

Permitting people in same-sex marriages to be ordained and serve as ministers

The problem with the bishops' third proposal is that, just like the previous two proposals, allowing clergy to be in same-sex marriages would contravene two parts of Church of England doctrine, both of which reflect the teaching of the visible Christian Church as a whole since New Testament times.

The first part is the requirement outlined in the 1662 Ordinal that those who are ordained should be persons of 'godly conversation,' conversation here meaning way of life. In other words, while all those who are ordained will obviously be sinners, they should nevertheless be people whose way of life is such that it does not mark a deliberate rejection of the requirements for holy living set out in Scripture and upheld by the Church of England.

Canon C4.1 states similarly that:

> Every bishop shall take care that he admit no person into holy orders but such as he knows either by himself, or by sufficient testimony… to be of virtuous conversation and good repute and such as to be a wholesome example and pattern to the flock of Christ.

The conviction that ordained ministers ought to be people of 'virtuous conversation and good repute' is also reflected negatively in the statement in Article XXVI of the Thirty-Nine Articles that while the sacraments can be efficaciously administered by 'evil Ministers,' nevertheless:

> …it appertaineth to the discipline of the Church, that inquiry be made of evil Ministers, and that they be accused by those who have knowledge of their offences; and finally being found guilty, by just judgement be deposed.

'Evil Minsters' here includes those who are morally evil as well as those who teach heresy and the reason that the Article holds that they should, after a proper process of investigation, be removed from office, is to ensure that as far as possible only those ministers who do provide 'a wholesome example and pattern to the flock of Christ' remain in post.

The second part is the doctrine of the Church of England noted above that marriage has been established by God as a relationship between two people of the opposite sex, that any other form of marriage than that established by God is unlawful and that unlawful marriage is a serious sin for which those involved will have to answer to God on 'the dreadful day of judgement.'

What the bishops do not show, or make any attempt to show, in GS 2358 is how the change they are proposing in the requirements for ordination and the exercise of ordained ministry would not mark a departure from these two parts of existing Church of England doctrine. The point they entirely fail to address is that such a change would either be a departure from the Church's doctrine regarding the requirements for ordination, or it would be a departure from the Church's doctrine with regard to what constitutes 'virtuous conversation' in relation to marriage.

It is important to note that nothing in the Church of England's doctrine prevents the ordination of men and women who experience same-sex attraction. Whether or not someone is sexually attracted to members of their own sex is irrelevant to their suitability for ordination. What matters is their behaviour, whether their way of life is marked by 'godly conversation.'

Why this matters is because according to the doctrine of the Church of England the fundamental calling of an ordained minister is to declare in word and deed the good news of Jesus Christ and what it means to live rightly in response to it. They cannot do this effectively if their behaviour contradicts the message they are called to declare, and this is the case if an ordained minister is living in a same-sex marriage. As the biblical commentator Matthew Henry puts it, 'Those who teach by their doctrine must teach by their life, else they pull down with one hand what they build up with the other.'[9] A minister who does not provide a godly example by the way they conduct their personal life will necessarily undermine the good that they do by their teaching and preaching.

A Church of England minister who is in a same-sex marriage may be an excellent minister in other respects, but they will undermine the good they do in their ministry if by their personal life they convey the message that same-sex marriage is acceptable in the sight of God and thus potentially lead others into the sinful way of life into which they themselves have entered. To echo the language of Bishop Schneider quoted earlier, their way of life will constitute a 'scandal' to those to whom they are called to minister.

At heart this is a matter of love. The visible Church is called to show love, and this involves not simply affirming people as they are, but, when necessary, explaining why their lives need to change and how God's power makes this change possible. This was the kind of love that Jesus modelled in his earthly ministry, and it is the kind of love that the visible Church as his body must show too. Part of what it means to show this kind of love involves telling people that God has instituted marriage as a relationship between two people of the opposite sex and that all other forms of 'marriage' are (a) not marriage at all and (b) seriously sinful. And this message will not carry conviction

---

9   David Winter, ed., *Matthew Henry's Commentary, Acts to Revelation* (London: Hodder & Stoughton, 1975), 368.

unless it is modelled in the lives of the people within the visible Church, and particularly by its ordained ministers, in the form of life marked by either marriage or a life of sexually abstinent singleness. In consequence, the call to love necessarily involves the maintenance of the Church of England's existing discipline with regard to ordination.

What is also worth noting about the bishops' proposal to consider changing the Church's discipline with regard to ordained ministry is that only those in civil same-sex marriages would benefit from this change. Those in same-sex civil partnerships and other, more informal, same-sex partnerships would still be excluded.

This fact is significant because it seems to imply that civil same-sex marriages have a moral value in the eyes of the Church of England equivalent to that possessed by marriages between two people of the opposite sex. At the Reformation the Church rejected the Western medieval belief in compulsory clerical celibacy holding instead that it is 'lawful' (i.e, compatible with the law of God) for clergy 'to marry at their own discretion as they shall judge the same to serve better to godliness' (XXXII). What the bishops are now doing is to stretch the meaning of the term 'marriage' under the Article to include civil same-sex marriages in spite of the fact that according to Church of England doctrine these 'marriages' are not marriages at all.

By doing this the bishops would be giving same-sex 'marriages' an implicit acceptability within the Church of England that moves the dial towards a general acceptance of them ('if the clergy can be in same-sex marriages, why can't such marriages be celebrated in church?'). This again is a move away from Church of England doctrine and hence from unity in truth.

The bishops' call for additional study of doctrine

I have noted that the bishops have not given any justification for considering changing the Church of England's current discipline with regard to ordination. What they have said, however is that:

> ...we are proposing that theological advice is sought on the nature, role, and creation of doctrine from the Theological Adviser(s) to the House of Bishops and the Faith and Order Commission Episcopal Reference Group (FAOC ERG). This work will then resource the ongoing discernment period.

> This theological work will aim to provide clarity around how doctrine can develop or change within the Church of England: as a result of this, the House of Bishops will be able to make decisions on the question of the removal of restrictions on clergy entering same-sex civil marriage. It is envisaged that this theological work would be completed within a time frame to enable the House of Bishops consider decisions by January 2025.[10]

This proposal raises three questions.

10   *LLF: Moving Forward as one Church*, 10–11.

The first is why the timescale proposed for this study is so short. As someone who was the Secretary of the Faith and Order Advisory Group and then the Faith and Order Commission, and also the theological consultant to the House of Bishops from 2000–2013, I can say on the basis of years of first-hand experience that there is no way that the persons referred to can produce detailed, comprehensive, agreed advice to the bishops in time for the bishops to make a properly informed decision in January next year. Like the production of good wine, the production of worthwhile theological advice takes time, and in their haste to make a decision the bishops are not making that time available.

The second is why the bishops are only now wanting to know about the nature and development of doctrine. In a rational world the bishops would have taken steps to be clear about the sources, nature and development of doctrine *before* embarking on the whole LLF project. The reason for this is simple. Doctrine provides the basis for the Church's practice and so in order to make a properly informed decision about the Church's practice, in this case in relation to issues to do with marriage and human sexuality, you have to know what doctrine permits and what it rules out. Doctrine provides the parameters for the discussion. It tells you 'You may do this, and you may not do that.' In admitting, at least tacitly, that they are unsure what the doctrine of the Church of England is, the bishops have unwittingly called into question the entire legitimacy of the LLF project, which has been episcopally driven from the start. If they are saying, in effect, that they have had no clear idea of what they should be doing, then why should we have any confidence in the end result?

This leads to the third question, which is why it is that the bishops are now turning to the exploration of doctrine. What is it that they are hoping to achieve? The answer is provided, I think, by the list of doctrinal questions which the bishops say need to be explored. These questions are:

> ...how do we, as a church, develop or change our doctrine? Is it possible to hold multiple doctrines simultaneously, in order to respond in the most gracious and pastoral way possible, even when this is messy or incoherent? Is it possible for there to be a range of interpretations of one doctrine?[11]

It is the last two questions that are the key to understanding the bishops' motivation. The problem they are facing is that the majority of them want to change the current discipline about the lifestyle of the clergy, but they are aware that the doctrine of the Church of England appears to rule this out, for the reasons given above, and because they lack the necessary votes in Synod to change that doctrine by due synodical process. What they therefore want to be able to argue is either that the existing doctrine can stay in place, while a new liberal doctrine is held alongside it, or that the present doctrine can be understood in the traditional way, but also in a way that permits what they want to do.

_____

11   LLF: Moving Forward as one Church, 10.

To put it another way, they see doctrine not as an authoritative guide, but as an obstacle, and they are hoping to receive theological advice that will remove that obstacle. As a bishop once said to me when I was the bishops' theological consultant: 'theologians are like plumbers, their job is to remove blockages.' This is, of course, not what theologians are for. Their job is to be truth tellers, and this role may very often involve saying that obstacles are immovable, that it is not legitimate for someone to do what they want to do however much they may want to do it.

It is to be hoped that the theologians who have been given the task of exploring doctrine by the bishops, being honest people, will come back to the bishops and tell them that they cannot hold multiple contradictory doctrines simultaneously (because truth is one and not pluriform, which is why, for example, something cannot be black and white at the same time) and that the law of non-contradiction means that conflicting interpretations of the same doctrine cannot all be true and therefore authoritative for the Church's practice. This is something that the theologians concerned will be able to do in the time allotted to them, because if they are competent theologians this is something they will already know.

What all this means is that in spite of insisting that 'Unity matters – it really matters', what the bishops are doing says that in reality they think otherwise. Whatever it is that the bishops are seeking to achieve, it is not to maintain unity in truth, if truth is measured against what is taught in the sources of doctrine which the Church of England accepts, the Scriptures, the orthodox Fathers, Creeds and

Councils of the Church, and the Church of England's three historic formularies.

The question of discernment

A further thing that the bishops are proposing in GS 2358 is that there should be a period of 'discernment' which would act as a 'mechanism through which we might discern God's leading for the longer term.' This discernment would involve looking at how the blessing of same-sex couples (and potentially also the ordination of those in same-sex marriages) has worked in practice and considering how arrangement in relation to these matters might therefore develop in the future.

There are two reasons why this proposal should not be regarded with respect.

Firstly, the bishops say nothing about the criteria by which the discernment will take place. What precisely is being discerned and by what standard? They do not say.

Secondly, and more importantly, the idea that the process would 'discern God's leading for the longer term' is arguably a breach of the third commandment in Exodus 20:7 'You shall not take the name of the Lord your God in vain.' The point here is that the commandment is not just about casual profanity, but about not co-opting God's name in support of our own sinful agendas. That is what the bishops are proposing, the bishops are saying that God's leading should be sought in the development of a process which involves the rejection of his will as this has been made known though the sources of doctrine. It is about asking for God to guide the Church in the way of sin and that is something that the Church should never ever do.

The fundamental problem is content not procedure

A final point to note is that is important to be aware that the fundamental problem with what the bishops are proposing in GS 2358 is to do with the content of what they are proposing rather with the method they are proposing to bring it to pass. Following the publication of GS 2358, eleven Church of England bishops published an open letter in which they were critical of it and called on their fellow bishops to think again.

In this letter they state that they:

> ...do not believe that the proposals will protect our unity in mission to the nation or our partnerships within the wider Church. We are persuaded that a commitment to unity will instead be demonstrated by the resolve we show to take the time we need to achieve sufficient consensus in relation to doctrinal matters. This is why we continue to call upon our fellow bishops and General Synod not to set aside the proper canonical procedures for considering

theological and liturgical developments, which are intended to guard our unity.[12]

While their criticism of the bishops' bypassing the normal Church of England procedures for considering theological and liturgical developments is a valid one, the problem with their statement is that it implies that the only thing needed to protect unity is the building of consensus through following these procedures. However, as we have seen, what is needed to protect unity is in fact adherence to the truth taught in the Bible and witnessed to by the orthodox writings of the Patristic era and the historic formularies. Should the Church of England, following correct canonical procedures, reach a consensus to depart from this truth, true unity would not have been maintained. As Sandys noted, there can be just as much consensus in error as there can be consensus in truth.

What we really need from orthodox bishops is for them to follow the example set by Bishop Keith Sinclair in his dissenting statement opposing the 'Pilling report' of 2013 and to mount a proper theological critique of the bishops' proposals.[13] As guardians of the faith called to 'drive away all erroneous and strange doctrine contrary to God's Word; and both privately and openly to call upon and encourage others to the

---

12   *Premier Christianity*, 24 June 2024, 'Exclusive: Bishops call for LLF re-think for sake of unity' at: https://www.premierchristianity.com/exclusive-bishops-call-for-llf-re-think-for-sake-of-unity/17868.article.
13   'A Dissenting Statement by the Bishop of Birkenhead,' in *Report of the House of Bishops Working Group On Human Sexuality* (London: CHP 2013), 119–145.

same'[14] it is their basic episcopal calling to do this, but it is something they have not yet done.

---

14   1662 Ordinal, 'The Form of Ordaining or consecrating an Archbishop or Bishop.'

IV. How should faithful Christians in the Church of England respond to what the bishops are proposing?

Four principles for orthodox Anglicans

In thinking how to respond to what the bishops are proposing in GS 2358, there are four principles that need to be borne in mind.

The first principle is that even if what the bishops propose comes to pass, the Church of England will still be part of the visible Church.

Article XIX notes that the visible Church is susceptible to error and in similar fashion the Westminster Confession notes that visible churches 'are more or less pure, according as the doctrine of the gospel is taught and embrace, ordinances administered, and public worship performed more or less purely in them.'[1]

What this means is that the fact that the Church of England has become less pure because it has committed the error of accepting the bishops' proposals does not mean that it has ceased to be a part of the visible church of Christ. This would only be the case if it entirely ceased to be a community where the Christian faith is professed, where the Word is preached, and the sacraments are duly administered. There is no sign at the present that this will be the case.

---

1   *The Westminster Confession*, 22.

The second principle which follows from this, is that orthodox Christians still have a Christian obligation to continue to be in as much of a Christian relationship as possible with the other members of the Church of England even if they have fallen into error.[2]

The reason for this obligation is helpfully set out by the seventeenth-century Scottish theologian David Dickson in his book *Truth's Victory over Error*. In this book he addresses the question of whether Christians are obliged 'to maintain an holy fellowship' with other Christians who have become corrupt in their theology and/or manner of life. His response is that the example of Christ and the teaching of the Paul and John show that there are a number of reasons why they are obliged to do so:

> (1) Because the Church of the Jews in Christ's time was very corrupt, Matth. 15.7. Mark 6.7, 8, and yet both by his practice, and his command, he would not have his hearers to separate from it. For he both observed the feasts preached in their Synagogues: John 8.1, Luke 4.15. John 10.22. And he commands his hearers to observe what the Scribes and Pharisees bade them do, Matth. 23.2, 3. (2) Because the Apostle is so far from commanding separation from the Church of Corinth, that he praises their Meetings, (1 Cor. 5.4. 1 Cor. 11.20. 1 Cor. 14.23.) notwithstanding of the many gross scandals which were among them,

2   The language that has come to be used to describe this kind of relationship is the language of 'impaired communion.'

1 Cor. 1.11, 12, 13. 1 Cor. 5.1, 11. and 1 Cor. 15.12, 13. (3) Because the Apostle calls the Galatians, 'The Church of Christ, brethren and the children of God,' who were yet in some measure, removed from God, to another Gospel. Nay, says Paul, O foolish, (or senseless) Galatians, who hath bewitched you, (that is, so blinded the eyes of your understanding that ye cannot see the right truth, as the jugglers bewitch the outward eyes that men think they see that which they see not) that ye should not obey the truth; Gal 3.1. And yet since it was a constitute true Church, it was his judgement, there should be no separation from it notwithstanding of all the foresaid Faults. (4) Because the Church of Ephesus was a true Church, though they made defection from their first Love. So was the Church of Pergamos, though there were in it who held the doctrine of Balaam. So was the Church of Thyatira, notwithstanding that they suffered Jezebel, that called herself a prophetess, and taught the servants of Christ to commit fornication, and to eat things sacrificed to idols. (5) If we must separate from the Communion of the Church in things lawful, for the faults of others, or for the faults of Ministers, and if their sins pollute the worship of God to others, then we must not keep communion with any Church; seeing there can hardly be a Church where there are not some hidden Hypocrites:

nay, where there are not some, who are
known to be such by the Minister.[3]

The third principle is the one already emphasised
in this study that the Christian unity is bounded by
revealed truth. As Packer puts it:

> What God thinks and says is for
> Christians the absolute standard of
> truth. God spoke freely to reveal his mind
> about the realities of redemption and
> of redeemed life throughout the entire
> history of his redemptive work, from
> the days of Genesis to the days of Christ
> and his apostles some two millennia
> ago. That revelation is recorded and
> embodied in the canonical scriptures,
> which the Holy Spirit inspired so as to
> give the world every age an accurate
> knowledge and understanding of what
> God has said and done. What was thus
> revealed and recorded now stands over
> every human idea and cultural consensus
> to measure how far they are true or false
> by the yardstick of God's word. All who
> recategorize Holy Scripture as well-meant
> and insightful but factually unreliable
> human tradition, and assume the right to
> pass judgement on its truth and wisdom
> rather than letting it pass judgement
> on them, undermine Christian unity
> rather than advance it, and create huge
> confusion and vast spiritual uncertainty

3   David Dickson, *Truth's Victory over Error* (West Linn: Monergism Books, 2018) Kindle edition, Loc. 2540.

in the process. Little as controversy should be encouraged or enjoyed, those who would uphold the cause of Christian unity have to make clear the falsity of this intellectual method and its results, and must go on making it clear until (please God) this aberration becomes a thing of the past.[4]

If it is suggested that there are those who support the acceptance of same-sex relationships and yet still uphold the authority of Scripture, the response would have to be that they are in effect denying the authority of Scripture, even though they may not intend to do so, because they are reading it in a way that denies what God actually wishes to say through it.

The fourth principle is that showing love to other Christians as fellow members of the visible Church has to be undertaken in a responsible fashion that cannot simply involve an undiscriminating acceptance of all forms of behaviour, even when these are contrary to the revealed will of God. To quote Packer again:

Christian love for one another, as an expression of our unity in Christ, must be practiced responsibly, in light of what God has told us in Scripture and shown us in Christ about his ideal standards for human living. Failure to do this will disrupt Christian unity yet again. The idea that loving people – one's children, spouse, friends; disadvantaged and abused groups – means giving them

---

4   Packer, *Taking God Seriously*, 58.

73

everything they ask for and tolerating whatever they choose to do is a sad sub-Christian mistake. Love gives, certainly, but giving that does not observe the limits of behaviour acceptable to God and that does not, however indirectly, give encouragement and help towards self-control, emotional maturity, courage, humility, patience, truthfulness and trustworthiness, purity and holiness, and Christlikeness generally, is not Christian love in action. Moral insensitivity and indifference cancel Christian love, instead of expressing it. It is not loving, in the Christian sense, to confirm anyone, let alone fellow Christians, in wrong ways, and it is certainly not the way to acknowledge our Christian unity with anyone. Christian love is unconditional in the sense of accepting, respecting and showing goodwill to people just as they are, but it is not unconcerned or undiscerning about being beneficent as distinct from merely indulgent. True Christian love holds to Christian standards all the way.[5]

Holding these four principles together means that we have to recognise that:

a) The Church of England is a visible Church.

b) We therefore need to maintain as far as we can some kind of Christian fellowship to

---

5   Packer, *Taking God Seriously*, 59–60.

others who belong to it, regardless of their beliefs or manner of life.

c) We have to maintain the principle that the proper unity of the visible Church has to be bounded by what God has laid down in Scripture (and in the witness to Scripture borne by the other sources of Church of England doctrine).

d) We have to practice a form of Christian love that continues to witness to the standards for loving that God has revealed and does not simply affirm or indulge forms of behaviour that do not meet these standards.

The crucial question therefore becomes whether what the bishops propose will still allow a space within the Church of England for Christians who remain faithful to the traditional doctrine of the Church of England to continue to believe in, and live by, God's truth and God's standards for human conduct, and to teach others to do the same.

If the answer to this question is 'Yes' then they can with good conscience remain within the Church of England and encourage others to do likewise. If the answer is 'No' then the best thing for them to do would be to move to, or create, another visible Church where this is possible and to continue to maintain a faithful witness to those in the Church of England from there.

In summary, faithful Christians should seek to maintain fellowship with other members of the visible Church by remaining within the Church of England if at all possible, but the necessary conditions for them to remain need to be in place

The proposals for delegated episcopal ministry in GS 2358

What the bishops are proposing in GS 2358 in order to create these conditions is two things.

Firstly, orthodox clergy and parishes would not have to perform or permit prayers of blessing for same-sex couples either in normal services or in standalone services.

Secondly, if their diocesan bishop approved of the use of such prayers, and potentially also the ordination and licensing of clergy in same-sex marriages, orthodox clergy and parishes could receive delegated pastoral care from an orthodox bishop sharing their convictions, while still remaining under the overall oversight of their diocesan. It is proposed that symmetrical arrangement would be put in place for liberal clergy and parishes with a conservative diocesan.

The creation of provision for delegated pastoral care would also be accompanied by the creation of 'informal societies' which could: 'provide pastoral and spiritual support for parishes, ministers or individual lay people.'[6]

What the bishops are proposing can be seen to provide an immediate solution to the difficulties facing orthodox clergy and parishes.

6   LLF: *Moving Forward as one Church*, 10.

- They would not have to perform or allow prayers of blessing for same-sex couples.

- There would be a clear visible differentiation between the position of orthodox clergy and parishes and the teaching and practice of liberal diocesan bishops.

- Clergy and laity would be provided with some form of pastoral and spiritual support.

- If bishops exercising delegated episcopal ministry have responsibility for the selection of candidates for ministerial training and for the ordination, appointment and licensing of clergy and lay ministers, this would help to provide a pipeline for the provision of orthodox ministry into the future.

However, a number of significant problems still remain:

1. GS 2358 leaves the precise functions to be carried out by bishops exercising delegated episcopal authority as a matter for future discussion, thus leaving uncertain whether the functions delegated to them would be sufficient to supply the present and future needed of orthodox clergy and parishes.

2. Under the proposals the diocesan would still retain ordinary jurisdiction over all the parishes in a diocese and clergy and lay ministers would still have to be licensed by them and take an oath of canonical obedience to them. This could create real problems of conscience for some ministers and parishes.

3. The bishops float the idea that 'more formal, longer-term implementation (which may or may not include transferred oversight) could be considered' in the future. Such transferred oversight in which clergy and parishes would come under the ordinary jurisdiction of an alternative bishop would address the problem noted in (2) but there is no guarantee that it will be introduced.

4. The symmetrical nature of what is proposed would mean that orthodox diocesan bishops would have to permit same-sex blessings and the ordination and licensing of those in same-sex marriages within their dioceses even if they believed both things to be contrary to the will of God.

5. It is not clear how a sufficient supply of orthodox bishops to make the system work would be guaranteed in the future if the Church of England as a whole continued to move in a liberal direction.

6. There would be no legal guarantee that the arrangements would continue into the indefinite future rather than being eventually abolished under pressure from those who regarded them as enshrining discrimination against lesbian and gay people.

7. The current situation in the Church of England in which its doctrine and practice with regard to marriage and sexuality are increasingly at variance is unsustainable in the long term and there will be increasing pressure from both inside and outside to formally revise

B.30 to produce a 'gender-neutral' doctrine of marriage, and to permit same-sex marriages in church with a gender-neutral marriage liturgy.

8. Should the Church of England give in to such pressure and formally revise its doctrine, practice and liturgy, a scheme of delegated (or even transferred) episcopal provision would no longer be sufficient because orthodox clergy and parishes would not just be unable to accept the position of a particular diocesan bishop, but also the position of the Church of England as a whole.

9. The combination of 2–3 and 5–8 would be likely to make it increasingly difficult to persuade orthodox Christians to enter into Church of England ministry, thus exacerbating the serious shortfall in clergy numbers and candidates for ministry that already exists.

The alternative of a separate province for the orthodox

Because of these issues (and particularly the last one) what is required if the Church of England continues its present direction of travel is for the Church of England to agree as soon as possible to the creation of a separate province for the orthodox as already argued for by CEEC and the Alliance. This is what would give orthodox Christians confidence that they have a long-term future in the Church of England.

As CEEC has argued in its paper *Visibly Different*, such a province, which could be created by means of the

Dioceses, Pastoral and Mission Measure 2007,[7] would be in line with the existing ecclesiology of the Church of England,[8] which is already a federation of two separate provinces linked by a joint legislative body in which the Convocations and Houses of Laity of the two provinces meet together to make decisions about matters of common concern and to enact laws in the shape of measures and canons.

Such an orthodox province would have its own archbishop and other bishops, its own convocation, and its own code of Canon law, and would be able to give robust long-term protection to clergy and parishes who wish to adhere to traditional Church of England teaching and practice and provide a base from which the re-evangelisation of the rest of the Church of England and the English nation might take place in God's good time. A sketch of what such a province would look like is provided in Appendix 1 below.

The creation of a province along these lines would be a second-best solution, the best solution being a return by the Church of England as whole to a clear and unequivocal acceptance of the traditional Christian

7   This measure can be found at https://www.legislation.gov.uk/ukcm/2007/1/contents.

8   The claim by the Bishop of Oxford that the creation of a third province 'undercuts the very essence of Anglican ecclesiology' is simply untrue. It is not essential to Anglican ecclesiology that there should only be two provinces in the Church of England. Furthermore, his criticism that a new province would create a 'church within a church' ignores the obvious fact that in ecclesiological terms each of the two existing provinces of the Church of England already constitutes a church in its own right. If there are already two existing churches, then why not three?

view of marriage and human sexuality, namely that marriage is between two people of the opposite sex and that to quote C S Lewis the two legitimate Christian options are 'either marriage, with complete faithfulness to your partner, or else total abstinence.'[9]

However, unless and until the Church of England returns to this position, a structural solution involving a separate province is the best way for orthodox Christians in the Church of England to maintain the four principles of unity set out earlier. They could continue to remain part of the Church of England and in some degree of fellowship with those in its other provinces, while at the same time being permanently free to believe, teach and live out the traditional doctrine of the Church of England with regard to marriage and human sexuality. Unity in truth to the greatest degree possible would thus be maintained.

---

9   C S Lewis, *Mere Christianity* (Glasgow: Fount, 1984), 86.

Appendix I. A sketch of the Province of Mercia

The formation of the Province

The Province of Mercia[1] would be established through a measure passed by General Synod and an Order in Council, the amendment of Canon C17 and the amendment of the Synodical Government Measure 1969. This legislation would contain a provision that it could not be repealed except with the consent of the province.

The province would come into being by means of parishes voting in their PCCs to leave their existing diocese and transfer to a diocese in the new province instead. To give the new province stability, parishes would not be able to return to their previous diocese for a period of ten years. Apart from that requirement, parishes would be free to move from the provinces of Canterbury and York to the new province, or to move back the other way.

The organisation of the province

Like the existing provinces of Canterbury and York, the new province would consist of parishes, deaneries, archdeaconries and dioceses. The number of dioceses that would initially be formed would obviously depend on how many parishes opted to join the new province, but one possible pattern would be for there

---

1   The use of the term Mercia is simply because of the need to call the province something. It is not a title that has any official standing among those calling for a third province.

to be initially four dioceses, one in the Southwest, one in the South and Southeast, one in the Midlands and East Anglia, and one in the North. Chaplaincies in Europe would come under the diocese for the South and Southeast.

Each diocese would initially have one bishop and one of these would be the archbishop of the province. There would be no fixed archiepiscopal diocese and the office of archbishop would subsequently be held by the senior bishop of the province.

A parish church in each diocese would be the cathedral. This would contain the bishop's chair and would be used for diocesan services such as the enthronement of the bishop, ordinations, and the renewal of ordination vows on Maundy Thursday. The diocese would be named after the location of the cathedral and the incumbent would carry the title Dean. There would be no cathedral chapter and when not being used for diocesan services the cathedral would act as a normal parish church.

The doctrine, law and liturgy of the province

The doctrine of the Province of Mercia would be that of the Church of England at the point of its formation, minus any elements that were supportive of same-sex relationships and gender transition. In order to publicly show its alignment with other orthodox Anglicans around the world, the province could formally declare its allegiance to the 2008 Jerusalem Declaration and its adherence to the Fundamental Declarations of the Global South Fellowship of Anglican Churches.

The law of the province would be that of the Church of England at the point of its formation

Minus any elements that did not apply to the new province (such as provision for Cathedral chapters) and any elements that were supportive of same-sex relationships and gender transition.

The liturgy of the province would be the 1662 *Book of Common Prayer*, the 1662 Ordinal and *Common Worship*. Any liturgy that had been introduced into *Common Worship* to mark same-sex relationships or gender transition would not be permissible.

Ministry in the province

The forms of ordained and lay ministry current in the Church of England would continue in the new province. Women would therefore be eligible to serve as deacons, priest and bishops. Parishes unable to accept the ministry of women as priest or bishops could request to come under the oversight of a male bishop who shared their convictions.

The Patronage system would continue in the new province. The rights of presentation held by bodies such as the Church Pastoral Aid Society and Church Society and by private individuals would remain unchanged. Rights of presentation belonging to a bishop or to the Dean and Chapter of a cathedral would be automatically transferred to the bishop of a parish's new diocese.

Candidates for ordained ministry would be selected using Bishops Advisory Panels. These would be organised by the Church of England Ministry Division as at present, but the selectors would be members of the new province. The dioceses would establish a list of approved colleges and courses for ordination training and might also establish their own training courses.

Clergy from the other provinces in the Church of England could transfer to serve in the new province subject to them being judged suitable by the bishop of the diocese concerned and subject to their personal life being in accordance with the requirements that clergy should not be involved in a sexual relationship outside (heterosexual) marriage and that gender transition would be a bar to ministry.

Because clergy in the province would be ministers of the Church of England they would continue to be eligible to serve as Anglican chaplains in hospitals, schools, prisons and the armed forces.

The governance of the province

The Province of Mercia would be governed by a Convocation consisting of the bishops and elected members of the clergy and an elected House of Laity.

The members of the Convocation and of the House of Laity would be members of the General Synod of the Church of England. They would speak and vote at Synod and the House of Bishops on matters of common concern to the Church of England as a whole. They would not speak on matters pertaining to the Provinces of Canterbury and York unless invited to do so and would not be able to vote on such matters.

Legislation passed by the General Synod would only apply to the Province of Mercia if there was specific agreement from the province that it should, with appropriate modifications if necessary. This would be similar to the way in which existing measures of the Church of England can be adopted with modifications for the Diocese in Europe, the Isle of Man and the Channel Islands.

The Convocation and the House of Laity would also form the Provincial Synod of the Province of Mercia. This would meet separately from the General Synod to consider matters concerning the province. It would have the same law-making powers as the General Synod, but could only create law on matters relating to the province.

Each diocese and deanery would have its own synod and there would be Diocesan Boards of Finance and Education. A Diocesan Board of Education would be necessary because church schools belonging to parishes that had become part of one of the new dioceses would be the responsibility of that diocese. Where church schools served both parishes in a new diocese and parishes in one of the old dioceses then there would need to be local arrangements to ensure that there was fair representation from both dioceses in the governance of these schools. This would be similar to the arrangements already in place in ecumenical schools.

It would be possible for dioceses of the Province of Mercia to reach agreement with dioceses in the other provinces to provide shared services on matters such as property maintenance, safeguarding, or legal services.

The dioceses in the new province would relate to the Church of England Pensions Board and the Church Commissioners in the same way as the dioceses in the provinces of Canterbury and York.

Establishment

The Province of Mercia would remain part of the established church. Parishioners would therefore continue to have the right to worship and to be baptised, married or buried in or from their parish church in the province in accordance with the law applicable within the province. Bishops in the province would be appointed by the king on the basis of names agreed by a Crown Nominations Commission consisting of representatives from the province. Legislation from the Provincial Synod would need to receive royal assent after having been considered by the Ecclesiastical Committee in Parliament.

Ecumenical Relationships

The Provincial Synod would decide whether the existing ecumenical relationships of the Church of England would apply on the basis of whether the theology and practice of the other churches involved was compatible with that of the province. Clergy from the Anglican Network in Europe could be granted permission to serve in the new province under the terms of the existing 1967 *Overseas and Other Clergy (Ministry and Ordination) Measure.*

In line with the Pauline principle that we should not say to other members of the body of Christ 'I have no need of you' (1 Corinthians 12:12–26) the creation of a new province along the lines sketched out above would mean that the Church of England could stay together, but in a way which respected the conscientious convictions on both sides and would prevent the Church of England fracturing entirely. It would also mean that at least one part of the Church of England would be able to maintain close links with the majority of Anglican churches round the world who would be unwilling to maintain ties with Anglicans in England who decide to accept either same-sex blessings, same-sex marriage or the ordination of those in same-sex relationships.

Also by Martin Davie

Bishops: A Concise Study summarises the key points of Martin Davie's major study *Bishops Past, Present and Future* (Gilead Books, 2022). It is designed to meet the needs of those who would like to know about the role and importance of bishops in the Church of England, but who would baulk at tackling the 800+ pages of the original book.

This concise study is published in the hope that it will help many in the Church of England, both ordained and lay, to think in a more informed fashion about how bishops should respond to the challenges and opportunities facing the Church of England at this critical point in its history.

In our Latimer Briefing series

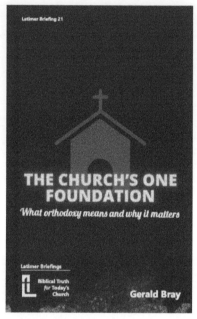

What is orthodoxy? In recent controversies in the Church of England and in the wider Anglican Communion, those who insist that the Church's traditional teachings about marriage and celibacy cannot be altered are increasingly described as 'orthodox', a claim that has been disputed on the ground that orthodoxy is defined by the great creeds and confessions of the Church, none of which mentions the subject.

This Briefing argues that orthodoxy extends well beyond what the creeds and confessions state. It is rooted in the mind of Christ, which is revealed to us in Holy Scripture and encompasses every aspect of life, including our doctrine and practice of matrimony.

Orthodoxy is expressed not only in creeds but also in the forms of our worship, not least in the rich tradition of hymnody that has stood the test of time. Christians of every tradition resonate with orthodoxy because it bears witness to the presence of the Holy Spirit in our hearts, as he illuminates and applies the Word of God to our lives.

Using the words of the well-known hymn *The Church's One Foundation*, Gerald Bray demonstrates what orthodoxy is and why it matters both to individual believers and to the Church as a whole. In every generation we are challenged by new heresies and divisions that seek to lead us astray. Orthodoxy is the unchanging teaching of Christ given to us in the Bible as the resource we need to combat them. It unites us with the saints of the past, the present and the future in the spiritual warfare that engages God's people as we make our way to the heavenly kingdom promised to all true followers of Jesus.

Also published by Latimer

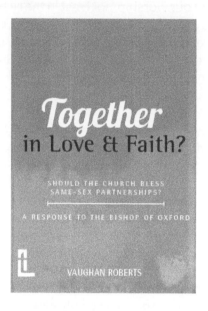

Writing from his own experience of same-sex attraction, Vaughan Roberts responds to the Bishop of Oxford's argument that the Church of England should change its doctrine and practice in relation to same-sex relationships. He outlines the beauty and goodness of the Bible's teaching on sex and marriage, as traditionally understood, and calls for it to be upheld with sensitivity and pastoral wisdom.

Milton Keynes UK
Ingram Content Group UK Ltd.
UKHW030802130824
446857UK00004B/71